Giant Panda

Nicole Boswell

Giant pandas live in mountain forests.

They are bears with black-and-white fur.

Their thick fur keeps them warm.

They have big, strong teeth.

They love to eat bamboo.

There are very few giant pandas still living in the wild.

 ears

 nose

 mouth

 paw